The Picnic Basket

by Joanne Mattern
Illustrated by Beatrice Bencivenni

Jayden and his brother Owen ran into the park. They had come with their family for a picnic and a concert. Lots of people were at the park that afternoon. Jayden helped Owen spread out the blanket. Then Mom and Dad opened the picnic basket and took out sandwiches and drinks.

Owen looked around. "Why do the baskets look so funny?" he asked.

The man on the next blanket leaned over and explained. "I guess you didn't know," he said. "The mayor is giving prizes for the best picnic baskets."

“Look at that cool basket,” said Jayden. “It looks like a pirate ship. And the family dressed like pirates!”

“What a creative idea!” said Mom.

"That family's basket looks like a race car!" Owen said, pointing to another family. He looked at his family's basket and frowned. "I wish our basket looked cool, too."

Jayden took some paper plates and napkins from the basket. Then he fished through his pockets, pulling out old crayons.

"Perfect! I'm glad I didn't throw these out," he said, smiling. "Now let's get to work!"

First, they made clown masks from paper plates. Next, they made silly hats out of napkins.

Last, Mom found a stick. She put the stick on the basket and hung the blanket over the basket.

The mayor came over to their blanket. “Your basket is a circus tent? What a great idea!” she said. The mayor pinned a bright ribbon on their basket. Jayden read it. “Most Creative Picnic Basket!” he said.

Mayor
CIRCUS
Most Creative
Picnic Basket

Jayden and Owen cheered. As the concert started, they sat back to enjoy their circus picnic.